printed in the United States by rocky heights print & binding

visit us at www.readkaleidoscope.com

kaleidoscope, *kids bibles reimagined*

library of congress cataloging-in-publication data is available upon request
ISBN
978-1-7360171-0-4 (paperback)
978-1-7360171-1-1 (hardback)

cover art by becca godfrey (www.beccagodfrey.com)
logo design by morgan carter (@bymorgancarter)
editing by sarah ammen

For my children
Jake, Caleb, Kate, and Charlotte
May you grow in wisdom as you grow in Jesus.

WELCOME TO KALEIDOSCOPE

First of all, thank you for picking up a copy of Kaleidoscope! We are glad to have you. In the following pages, you'll experience the Bible in a whole new way.

Kaleidoscope emerged from the need to retell the Bible for elementary-aged children at a level between a "little kid" Bible and an adult translation. In a way, we are a happy medium.

At Kaleidoscope, we are producing single volumes for every book of the Bible. We design them to read like chapter books, so you'll turn pages and look forward with anticipation to the next volume.

But don't let the fact that we are focused on kids deter you if you are a "big kid!" Good children's books are almost always as good for adults as they are for kids.

Get excited! In the pages that follow, you'll see God's fantastic good news. Our prayer is that his kindness, gentleness, and love will melt our hearts and make us more like Jesus.

Better than Gold takes the book of Proverbs, a book that's all about wisdom and yet so difficult to understand, and helps us see how it points to Christ. I'm so thankful for a kids Bible that not only offers my children more clarity, but that does the same for me as I read aloud to them! This is a fantastic resource for kids and parents alike.

-Hunter Beless (@hunterbeless, @journeywomenpodcast), Founder and Executive Director of Journeywomen and the host of the Journeywomen Podcast

We all want our kids to grow in wisdom, especially when all sorts of voices are coming at them with truth claims. Kaleidoscope gives kids the true source of wisdom—God's word. And points them to Jesus, the truly wise one.

-Courtney Reissig (@courtneyreissig), author
Teach Me To Feel: Worshipping Through the Psalms in Every Season of Life

One of the challenges of the book of Proverbs is tying seemingly random subjects together in a way that points consistently to the grace God has given us through Jesus. Our kids need to hear these riches, but not in a way that tells them, "God will love you if you can just be a good boy or girl." Kaleidoscope has captured the gospel in a really profound way.

-Dr. Jimmy Agan, Senior Pastor - Intown Community Church, Atlanta

This incredible resource equips parents to disciple their children with a biblical understanding of life's most common experiences. Each section ends with a gospel presentation, inherently teaching children and parents alike how to apply the gospel to everyday life, compelling them by the beauty and wonder of Christ to grow in wisdom.

-Lauren Weir (@wordsworthnoting), M.A. Biblical Counseling from SEBTS, co-owner Words Worth Noting, www.wordsworthnoting.com

Better Than Gold helps children understand how the gospel provides a foundation and a framework for walking in wisdom. Instead of feeling like they'll never be able to obey God, children will walk away from this book with practical ways to apply the gospel to every area of life. They will be compelled to treasure wisdom because they will see how Jesus—the perfectly wise One—is better than gold.

-Lauren Washer (@laurenwasher), wife, mom of six, and writer, www.laurenwasher.com

The things I long for my children to have are a strong faith in Jesus Christ as their savior and wisdom to follow the leading and instruction of the Lord. This precious retelling of Proverbs does just that. Jesus is always in view while showing your children the joy of Biblical wisdom. This is an excellent resource for your family!

-Korrie Johnson (@goodbookmom), Christian book reviewer, www.GoodBookMom.com

CREATORS

Chris Ammen is the founder of Kaleidoscope and a Children's Pastor in Tuscaloosa, AL. He has a BA and M.Ed. in Elementary Education as well as an M.Div. from Covenant Seminary. When not writing, Chris loves spending time with his wife, Sarah, and their four awesome kiddos!

Sabrina Newsome resides in Texas where she works as an artist. Sabrina's true passion lies in illustrations with a focus on portraits and cartoons. You can always catch Sabrina trying new vegan recipes, taking care of her many, many plants, exercising, drawing, and taking unnecessarily long naps.

TABLE OF CONTENTS

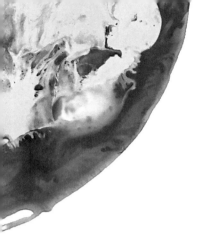

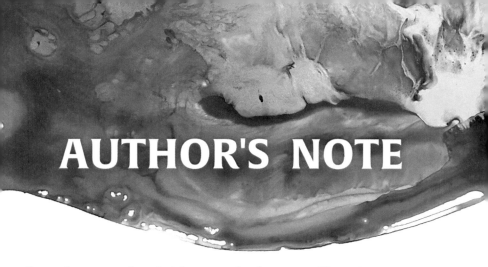

AUTHOR'S NOTE

If you have read Kaleidoscope before, you'll notice something different in this volume!

Typically, with a book like Acts or Judges, there is a storyline to follow. This makes it easier to retell the stories in the order you would read them in the Bible, just in elementary language.

The book of Proverbs is a bit different. There is no story. Instead, Proverbs is a collection of wisdom writings. It is rich, deep, and an essential part of how God speaks to his people.

But Proverbs also repeats itself a lot and doesn't fit the mold of other books in the Bible. The primary goal of Kaleidoscope is to retell the Bible at an elementary level. We look at each book to help kids get the most understanding from each of our volumes.

So, *Better Than Gold* is a book about Proverbs. It includes personal stories and references to other parts of the Bible. In these stories and references, you'll find the words of Proverbs. Instead of working straight through the whole book, we divided Proverbs into topics such as honesty, money, and justice.

We hope this approach will help you and your children walk away with a better understanding of Proverbs and a clearer picture of Jesus.

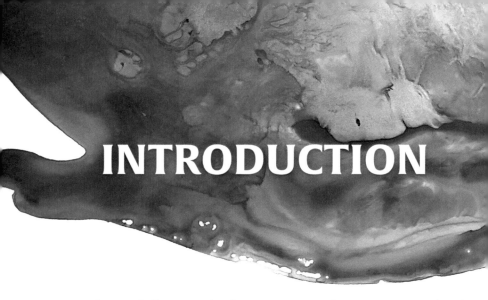

INTRODUCTION

How do we follow God when so many things seem to lead us away from Him? Put another way, how do we gain wisdom, the skill of Godly living, in a world full of sin? If you've ever asked these questions, or ones like it, the book of Proverbs is for you!

The fact is, when our first parents, Adam and Eve, fell into sin in the book of Genesis, the world broke. Life simply does not work the way it's supposed to. Instead of telling the truth, we tell lies. Instead of defending the weak, we take advantage of people. Instead of life, we see death almost everywhere we look.

The Bible tells us that even the creation - mountains, trees, and birds - know the world is broken by sin and are painfully groaning as they wait for Jesus to return. Proverbs says this longing is finally and fully satisfied in the most fantastic way possible - through Jesus, God's own Son.

All through Proverbs, we will see glimmers of Jesus. The Bible even tells us that Jesus is the "true wisdom of God." Jesus lived life perfectly in a broken world. Then He died for all the ways our lack of wisdom leads to sin.

The good news for us is that Proverbs was not written by perfect people. In fact, King Solomon, who wrote Proverbs*, continually broke God's law. Proverbs is not for flawless people. Instead, it was written for sinners living in a broken world who need help.

You'll never make God love you more or less by growing in wisdom. The gospel doesn't work like that. Jesus died for all of your sin - past, present, and future.

If you look at wisdom as something you must get to make God love you, life will be very stressful! You'll think, "Have I done enough? Have I done the right things? I feel like I still have so far to go!"

But if you believe what the Bible says about your sin and the forgiveness you can have through Jesus, then you'll know that God already loves you.

When God looks at you, he sees all of Jesus's wisdom and none of your foolishness. You don't have to make God happy. God likes you. He is already as happy with you as He will ever be. He is so glad about you that his angels sing about you in heaven!

*Most people think Proverbs is a collection of writings, with Solomon as the main writer. But, to make things simple, we'll just use Solomon's name throughout this book.

Only when you know deep down that God is not mad at you or expecting you to act a certain way to earn your way into heaven will you see wisdom as something wonderful. Then wisdom becomes something you want.

Now, you should know that wisdom does not come easy. At first, wisdom is like a map that we have to look at all the time to understand where we are going. But over time, with prayer and practice, the skill of wisdom becomes more a part of who we are.

And this wisdom in Proverbs is for everyone, including kids! So, let's dive in together!

WISDOM & FOOLISHNESS

Just the other day, one of my friends said something really mean to me. It hurt. A lot.

Has this ever happened to you?

Of course it has. Perhaps you, too, have said something unkind to someone. Unfortunately, pain and hurt are a part of life.

We don't have to wonder if hard things will happen to us. We know difficulties will come. The big question is: What will we do when life hurts?

On the other hand, we should ask, "What will I do when life is spectacular?" When I win the big game, make a lot of money, or feel deeply loved. What will I do in those moments? Will I give thanks to God or think my life is great simply because I'm awesome?

For these and many other reasons, the Bible says we need to grow in something called wisdom. Wisdom is skill in Godly living.

You can be skilled in lots of things. You might know how to catch a great, big fish. You might be a great dancer, a math whiz, or a basketball superstar. But God says the most important skill is knowing how to live life well, knowing the best thing to do in the millions of moments He puts us in every day.

In the book of Proverbs, we learn lots about wisdom. Solomon, the book's writer, asks this question near the beginning, "How much is wisdom worth? Is it more valuable than silver and hidden treasures? My child, I tell you it is worth more than all the silver and treasure in all the world!" Later in the book, Solomon says wisdom is even better than gold! Nothing can compare!

Solomon spends the whole book of Proverbs telling us that wisdom is so important that we must call out and look for it. When we find wisdom, we must bottle it up and get as much of it as we possibly can!

Only when you seek wisdom will you truly begin to respect the Lord. Only then will you find the knowledge of God.

But get this, you cannot simply get wisdom from anywhere as if it were hanging around every corner. You cannot buy it like a candy bar. You cannot build it like a tree house. Wisdom comes only from the Lord. He gives it to those who ask Him, not because you deserve it, but simply because He loves you as His child.

You'll notice, though, that God has a name for those who are not wise and live life any way they want. He calls them *fools*. Other places in Proverbs, he calls them *evil* or *scoffers*. The point is that there are two ways to live in this world. You can follow God and grow in wisdom. Or you can follow anything or anyone else, and grow in foolishness.

Foolishness is not something we can easily get rid of.

When making bread, one of the first steps is to grind the wheat to separate the bad parts from the good. The Bible says you can grind a foolish person like you would grind wheat, but they will still be foolish.

We don't need a tool or better behavior to get rid of foolishness; we need a rescuer, Jesus.

So how does this work itself out in real life?

Remember when my friend said something really mean to me? It hurt. A lot. Out of my hurt, my sinful heart wanted to hurt him back. I wanted to punch him! But that would have been foolish. He may have hurt me with his words, but hurting him with my hands would have just made things worse.

Thankfully, because God is at work growing wisdom in me, I remembered the gospel - the ultimate source of all wisdom.

What is the gospel?

Just like my friend hurt me with his words, I hurt God's heart with my sin. The Bible says my sin deserves the punishment of death.

But God did not and will not give me what I deserve. Instead, God sent His only Son, Jesus, to die for me. God did this so He could call me a child of God. God is not angry with me. I am forgiven. That is the gospel.

Right in the middle of the gospel, we find Jesus. The Bible tells us that Jesus not only died for our sin, but He is also the "true wisdom of God" (1 Corinthians 1:30). If both of these things are true, then the wisdom I am growing in must be shaped by the gospel.

So when people hurt me with their words, I remember how God treats me when I hurt Him. That doesn't mean I let people walk all over me, continually hurting me. No, sometimes we have to distance ourselves from harmful people.

But this time, I was able to offer kindness and show my friend more of Jesus. I told him how he made me feel and forgave him. He apologized, told me he didn't mean it, and said, "I'm sorry."

Wisdom caught my anger like a net and led me to respond in a way that reflected what God wants for His kingdom.

This book will be like a journey into what it means to live in light of what Jesus has done for us and how that helps us grow in wisdom.

Come along! This will be fun!

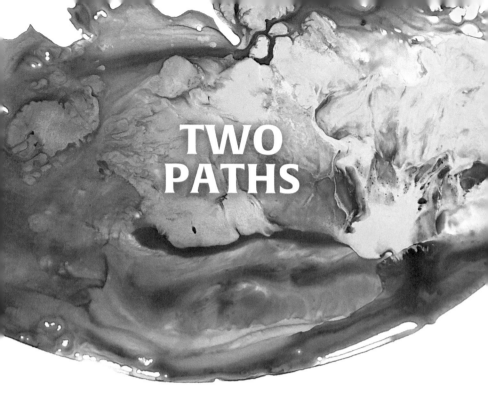

TWO PATHS

In Proverbs, Solomon often speaks to kids just like you! He says things like, "Children, listen to these words. I, too, was once young. I was a child in my parent's house. They loved me dearly, and so when my father said, 'Store up these words in your heart,' I listened closely."

"So now I tell you, get wisdom and understanding. Get as much of it as you can! Wisdom will bring you a full and fruitful life."

"Value wisdom highly. Get it at all costs. Wisdom will be like a beautiful crown on your head. It will be your honor and your protection."

Then, Solomon gives us these two really helpful pictures of wisdom. First, he says wisdom is like a lovely, safe path. When you walk, nothing will slow you down or make you trip.

Wisdom leads you to joy and delight. Walking in wisdom is like walking hand in hand with God. So, while life won't always be perfect, growing in wisdom will make life a lot better!

But, the way of the foolish is much different. Their path is full of deep darkness and evil. Everything is hidden and full of shame. Don't kid yourself. Even if you only explore their path a little, you will grow in sin. Evil people live along foolish paths, and they will not sleep until they have made you like one of them.

But the path of those who do right is like the sun in the morning. It shines brighter and brighter until the full light of day. Nothing is hidden! Everything is seen and celebrated!

If you walk with God, look straight ahead at the beauty in front of you! Don't let anything take you from the way of wisdom. Think deeply about the path your feet walk. Do not swerve to the right or to the left. Turn your feet away from evil, and you will have life to the fullest!

But this is not the only picture of wisdom Solomon gives us. As we walk, we will grow hungry and need to eat!

TWO MEALS

What is your favorite meal? Imagine all the delightful tastes and smells. Whether it's a home-cooked lasagna or a hamburger from McDonald's, there is nothing quite like your favorite food!

In Proverbs, Solomon tells a short story to open our minds, hearts, and taste buds to wisdom. The star of the story is a woman who is actually named *Wisdom*. She lives in a beautiful, strong house. Wisdom has set out a delicious meal with mouthwatering meats and tasty drinks.

But her food was not just for those living in her house. Instead, Wisdom climbed to the highest point of the city, raised her voice, and called, "Let all who are childish come to my house. Come, eat, and drink! Leave your childish ways and find life with me! Walk in the way of understanding."

If you go to Wisdom's house and eat with her, she will teach you how to live with skill in a broken world. Wisdom will teach you to honor the Lord. Wisdom will bring you understanding that flows like rivers of life.

Wisdom, though, is not the only character in this story. Another woman, in another house, is named *Foolishness*. She is wild and knows only evil.

Foolishness sits at the door of her house and at the highest point of the city. She calls out to all who pass by, "Let the childish come to my house instead! But do not tell anyone where you're going. Food eaten in secret tastes so delicious."

But unlike Wisdom's food and drink, this meal leads to death, not life. In fact, Foolishness's house is filled to the brim with dead people who appear to have life.

A lot is going on in this story! Picture these two homes, these two meals, these two women. Which meal would you want to eat? The choice, I hope, is clear!

But there is even more here than meets the eye! One day, Jesus will announce a greater meal, a better meal.

In the book of Revelation, the last book of the Bible, John writes that Christians everywhere will share a meal with Jesus, the true wisdom of God.

At that meal, Jesus will be the groom, the Lamb of God. He is the one who has given His life for His bride. We are pictured as the bride, who has prepared herself for her husband by dressing in fine linen clothes. The clothes, the Bible says, are the righteous deeds of the saints.

But these clothes are not our own. We did not stitch them together or buy them at the store. Instead, the clothes are a gift from the groom. Jesus' righteous deeds, which are His perfect life, wisdom, death, and resurrection, become as if they were ours.

All our foolish ways, all of our sin, all of our lack of wisdom is gone. When we trust Jesus, God sees us as He sees His own Son!

Proverbs invites us to come to Wisdom's home because one day we will dine with the true wisdom of God, Jesus. God wants us to begin tasting the meal we will eat, finally and fully, when Jesus returns. What a glorious invitation! Will you hear Jesus calling out to you and join Him at the table?

HONOR THE LORD

If you read Proverbs in your mom or dad's Bible, you may see a phrase that will seem quite scary at first: "The fear of the Lord is the beginning of knowledge."

Fear?!

You might be afraid of snakes...but is the Lord someone like that to be scared of too? This is a great question! The good news is the answer will help us see that God is really more loving than we could ever imagine.

When the Bible uses the word *fear*, it has much more to do with honor and respect. But there is still some fear wrapped up in honor and respect!

The reason you might keep your distance from a snake is that you honor and respect the fact that the snake could bite you. You don't act any old way you want to around a snake because you know what could happen! In a way, your fear of the snake has brought you knowledge.

Fear also reminds me of a time when I was eight years old. I wanted so badly to be a professional basketball player! One day, in a hotel lobby, I ran right into Scottie Pippen. Scottie was a famous player for the Chicago Bulls, the best team on the planet at the time. I was so nervous about meeting Scottie that I almost couldn't find the words to talk to him!

When you find yourself in front of someone you respect so much, you tremble. You might even feel a little nervous. But it's not a bad feeling. It's because you admire the person you're with so much.

This is what the fear of the Lord is. It's a good fear that you will disappoint or dishonor the person. Good fear is all about love.

This type of fear will make you wise. Here's how...

When I ran into Scottie Pippen, there were lots of other people around. But I couldn't tell you what they looked like. However, I can tell you to this day that Scottie was wearing an off-white suit with a black shirt.

The good fear I had around Scottie made everything else matter a whole lot less! At that moment, I only cared what Scottie thought of me and what I thought of Scottie.

In a similar way, the fear of the Lord makes us wise because it makes everything else seem less important. Toys, money, popularity, grades, and approval. All of these and more begin to lose importance as the light of God shines brighter in our lives!

Fear of the Lord also makes us satisfied with what we have. Proverbs says it is better to respect the Lord and have a little money than to have lots of money and not fear God. Money will not last, and if we love it more than the Lord, our lives will be miserable.

Solomon also tells us that if we have a growing fear of people instead of an increasing fear of the Lord, we will be miserable.

If your goal in life is to keep everyone around you happy, you'll actually end up being unhappy. What people want from you will become a never-ending, moving target. Sometimes you will hit it, and you'll feel good for a moment. But most times, you will not live up to others' expectations and grow worried about what they think of you.

Solomon tells us that if we trust in the Lord, He will keep us safe. Here's how...

You see, if we spent our whole lives trying to make God happy, it would be a never-ending, moving target. We would never hit the bullseye perfectly every time and live up to His holy standards.

But one person hit the target without fail. Jesus. God's own Son lived the life we should have lived, perfect and spotless. And then God gave the punishment we deserve for our sin to His Son.

Jesus was put in harm's way so that we can be safe.

When we see what God has done for us, it makes us love Him. It makes us tremble in His presence. Without Him, we would deserve what happened to Jesus. But God is kind, gracious, and merciful. He loves you. He is not mad at you.

His love for us makes us fear the Lord. That makes us honor and respect Him. That makes everything else fade in importance as He becomes the only one who truly matters.

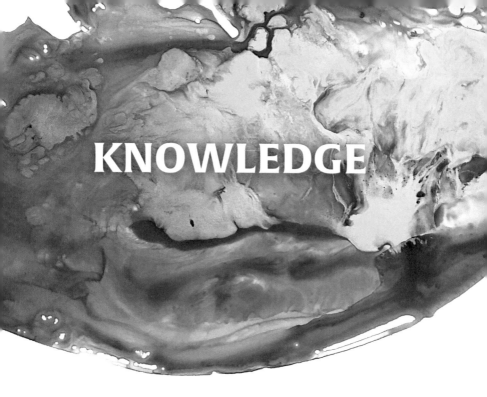

KNOWLEDGE

What are you learning right now? You go to school to learn about cool things like sparklemuffins (look it up, it's crazy!). You might go to a sports practice to grow in your soccer skills. You might even be learning how to create beautiful paintings. All of us grow in knowledge every day.

Proverbs tells us that people who trust in the Lord are blessed and happy. Why is that? The Bible says it's because they are not only learning about sparklemuffins but are also growing in a special type of knowledge: the knowledge of God.

When you grow in knowing God, you learn more and more about what God did to make you His child. You could spend the rest of your life and never get to the bottom of the simple truth that God sent His one and only Son to die for you. His love is just that wonderful!

As we grow in the skills we need to live in God's world, we continue to grow in knowledge. Solomon says that a heart that understands what is right is on the lookout for knowledge. People like this walk straight ahead, with their eyes on the Lord. But, he says, foolish people's eyes are always looking around for the next thing to make them happy.

Where do you get this knowledge? The Bible says to look to God's word. Proverbs says that every word of God is perfect and is like a shield to those who learn from it.

After the Bible, we listen to others who know God, have studied the Bible, and share their wisdom with us. Proverbs tells us that those who pay attention to what they're taught will have success in life.

As we grow, we tuck wisdom deeply in our hearts so our life becomes like a refreshing spring in the middle of a city. This only happens as we carefully listen to words of wisdom and knowledge when they come our way.

But, listening to the wisdom of others is not quite as easy as it sounds. If we are really learning how to live skillfully in God's world, we will soon discover we haven't figured out life as much as we thought!

Listening well often means admitting we are wrong or that we don't have all the answers. In fact, Proverbs says those who think they have answers before listening to others are foolish.

When we grow in our knowledge of God, we become refreshing to be around. Through the rest of this book, we will talk about what it means to grow into someone who listens to wisdom, knowing it comes from and points us towards God's true wisdom: Jesus.

CREATION

What do you love about God's world? You may picture the birds and trees. Maybe you think of the sun and the moon. Isn't it glorious to think of all that God has made?

But, did you know that before God made the very first star in the sky, He made wisdom? As you know by now, Jesus is called the "true wisdom of God." Jesus was with His Father as they created the world.

Proverbs says it beautifully.

Before there were any oceans or flowing streams of water, wisdom was born.

Before the mountains nestled into their places and the hills rose up from the ground, wisdom was there.

Wisdom watched as the dust of the earth was scattered and as fields sprung to life.

As heavens were set in place, wisdom looked on with joy!

At the place where the sky meets the sea, wisdom sat and smiled.

When the clouds puffed in the sky above, when the oceans filled with water, God poured wisdom into all creation.

As the Lord set the foundations of the earth, wisdom was at His side. Wisdom was delighted to be with God, and God was delighted to be with wisdom.

Those who find wisdom, find life itself because wisdom was here before life began. Every living creature longs to taste even a hint of it. When they do, life flows into the very place wisdom made.

Wisdom was knit into the fabric of the world. There, wisdom grew strong and immovable, like a tree. Wisdom's roots sunk deep into the earth. When winds blow and waters rage, wisdom stands firm.

So it is with those who seek after wisdom. They become like trees, which grow strong and cannot be easily moved from the land.

Those who grow in wisdom become more of who God made them to be, full of strength and beauty.

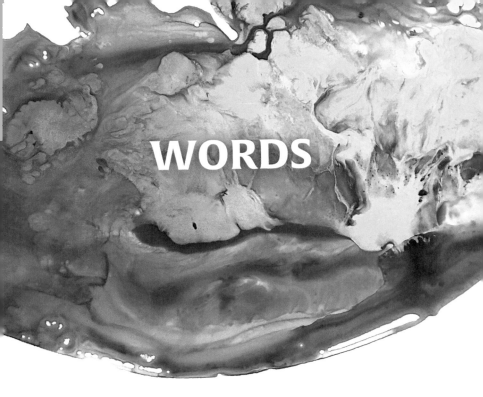

WORDS

Few things in life can make us feel crummier or chummier than the words we hear and speak.

To someone we love, we might say, "You're the coolest!" It fills both of you all the way to the brim with joy!

But, as you know, we can also use our words to hurt people. Proverbs tells us that our speech is really, really important. Words can be like honey, bringing life and healing. But, when used the wrong way, words can sting like a whip.

Ouch!

Living with skill in God's world is knowing the power of our words.

We can also hurt others with our words by lying. Solomon says that our words can be like a mask we use to hide behind. When we "put on our masks," we are following in a long line of hiders. Ever since Adam and Eve sinned in the Garden of Eden, we have been crafty and deceitful in trying to hide behind our lies from God and one another.

Not only do we lie, but we also gossip. We gossip when we spread news about someone that makes them look bad. Why do we do this?

Maybe we like the way it makes us feel: powerful, popular, or prettier. Proverbs even says that gossip is like tasty little bits of food. We love to nibble on cookies or munch on candy because it makes us feel good for a moment.

But if candy and cookies are all you eat, your tummy will not thank you for very long. You'll end up feeling sick! What you choose to eat will come back and bite you! The same goes for your words; they have the power to bring life or death, both to you and others. So be careful what news you choose to share!

As destructive as words can be when used poorly, they are like confetti raining down at a party when used the right way! A gentle, kind, thoughtful word can be like a tree of life to someone - refreshing, nourishing, and energizing.

Lips that speak kindness to others are like a priceless jewel. Think about that for a moment. You can spend all your money on the fanciest diamond, and yet a well-spoken complement or a kindly written note to a friend can mean more than all the jewelry in all the world!

Words can lift you up and make you feel more alive than ever. But, they can also drag you into a pit of despair. Why is this?

Words, as it turns out, have been important since the beginning of the Bible.

Think about this. In the beginning, God created everything. He didn't do it with a set of tools or a magic wand. No. He did it with words. He spoke, and the sun rose for the first time. He spoke, and the trees did their first happy dance, swaying in the wind!

But, there was another speaker at the beginning of the Bible. Satan. He questioned Adam and Eve, "Does God really love you?" These hurtful words sunk into Adam and Eve's hearts and poisoned all their children, including you and me, with sin.

Thankfully the story does not end there! God gave Jesus a special name. He called His one and only Son, *the word*. This means that Jesus is the truth about God.

All our lying, hateful, stinging words are swallowed up in the truth of God found in Jesus. How?

Proverbs says our words can bring healing to the body. Jesus, the true wisdom of God, came to earth and healed people in even more magnificent ways with only a word.

At the end of His life, Jesus was hung on a tree. Proverbs tells us that our words can be like a tree of life. But Jesus, when He was hanging on the tree of His death, spoke words of life, saying, "Father, forgive them."

Those words are like a tree of life. They heal those who believe what the Bible says about Jesus.

Jesus was wounded. He was beaten and whipped on the cross so that He can begin to heal our wounds from all the words that have whipped and bruised us.

When we know that we have been loved in this way, God will give us the power to love others. Only then will we become the type of people who speak with honesty, gentleness, and kindness to those around us. With our words, we can show the world that the kingdom of God is truly sweeter than honey and better than gold.

HONESTY

When I was about six or seven years old, I told a lie that I'll never forget.

On occasion, my brother and I would go to the grocery store with my mom. She would often give each of us a list of items to get. Once we found something on our list, we would put it in the cart, and then get the next item. I suppose it was a way to keep us kids busy. You know how parents are!

On one of these trips, a yummy treat caught my eye: a big cake with green jello on top! I wanted that cake so badly!

After pleading with my mom to get it and hearing "No!" for what seemed like the millionth time, I stormed off and came up with a plan. If I couldn't bring the cake home, perhaps I could just eat a little in the store, and nobody would notice.

I snuck back to the cake, pealed the lid back, took a bite, and then quickly fled the scene of the crime. It tasted so sweet! I can still remember it 30 years later.

But the cake did not taste good for very long! A store employee was watching the whole time. I thought no one knew, but she did, and she told my mom.

My mom bought the cake, and we took it home. As you can imagine, she was not happy! But she let me eat the cake.

All of it. All at once.

I was so sick to my stomach. My lie made the cake taste terrible!

In Proverbs, Solomon tells us that, "Food gained by cheating and lying tastes sweet. But in the end, you will end up with a mouth full of gravel."

How true this was for me! Lying rarely gets us what we want and usually leaves us feeling terrible.

The Bible talks a lot about truthfulness because sin wants to hide, and we lie to keep it hidden.

Maybe we lie because we don't trust that God will actually take care of us. When God came to Adam and Eve in the garden after they ate from the forbidden tree, they both lied. Would God take care of them even though they disobeyed? Adam and Eve were not so sure.

You can find people lying throughout the Bible. Abraham, Moses, Aaron, Saul, and David were all liars. In fact, it is harder to find someone who is always honest in the Bible than to find someone who chose to lie!

Even some of Jesus's closest friends, His disciples, lied. Judas turned his back on Jesus. Peter was dishonest and denied knowing Jesus three times!

But the Bible tells us that honesty makes life better. Proverbs says that honest people build up their city and cause it to be a better, happier, and more joyful place to live.

Honest people are healthy people, as healthy as a green budding plant. The fruit they bear gives life to those around them.

This picture of honesty building a city and being like a tree of life may sound cool enough. But, did you know it is actually telling us a bigger, better story?

As you know, our dishonesty is sin. It deserves death. But Jesus made a way for us to have true and lasting life. He lived a perfectly honest life and then died the death we deserve for our dishonesty.

Then, He was resurrected three days later and now lives in heaven with His Father. One day He will build what the Bible calls the new heavens and new earth. When this happens, all that is broken, shameful, hurtful, and yes, dishonest on earth will be fixed and made right again. In a way, it will be like the Garden of Eden all over, except much better.

Instead of a garden, God will build a city that will never be destroyed. It will have streets of gold, walls of jewels, and beauty unlike we have ever seen.

And guess who will be in the middle of the city? Jesus. From His throne will flow a river of crystal clear water. On both sides of that river, the roots of the tree of life will grow. It will bear fruit every season. Its leaves will give healing to all people.

Healing from our sin. Healing from our dishonesty and the pain it brings. What a gorgeous image!

Today, though, we do not live in a world with streets of gold and walls of jewels. But, we show the world glimmers of God's beautiful future when we live honestly.

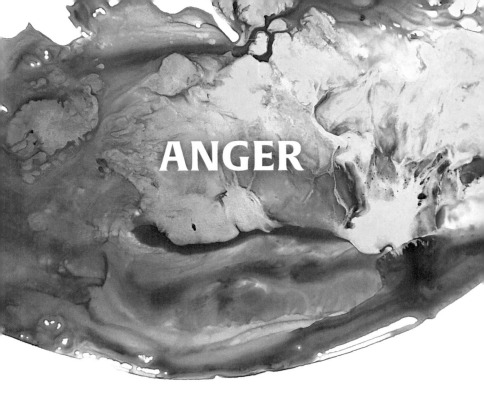

ANGER

What makes you who you are? Maybe it's your blue eyes, brown skin, or curly hair. You might be from Texas or Norway or even Just Room Enough Island (look it up; it really does exist!).

All of this is really important, but there is something much deeper about you that God knows and cares about.

Your heart.

Not the blood-pumping organ in your chest - although God certainly cares about that, too! When the Bible talks about your heart, it's talking, among other things, about your emotions. How are you doing? Is life beating you down or lifting you up? Are you angry, glad, sad, lonely, or fearful? Are you tired or energized?

Your emotions tell you much more about who God made you to be and how you are experiencing life in God's world than if your eyes are brown or green. Proverbs says it this way: "When you look at your reflection in the water, you see what your face looks like. But, when you look at your heart, you see what you are really like."

Proverbs tells us that a heart is like two sides of a coin. A peaceful, happy heart brings life to the body and makes a face look cheerful.

But the other side of the coin isn't quite so pleasant. A heart overcome by foolishness does quite the opposite. Solomon says that jealousy can feel like your bones are rotting, and a sad heart breaks your spirit.

You've probably had both kinds of feelings. When our spirits are high, it can seem like we can take on the world! But when life gets hard and our spirits fall, we can feel exhausted, and our bodies might even hurt.

One of the hardest emotions we deal with is anger. Proverbs reminds us that stones are heavy, and bags of sand weigh a lot. But walking through life angry is a heavier load than both. It is tiring and painful!

Anger has a way of taking root deep down in our hearts. It grips and overpowers us. We can feel crushed under anger's weight, unable or unwilling to take the next step.

Anger can stop us in our tracks. But it can also make us explosive, mean, or harsh. We can grow a bad temper that stirs up conflict around us. When we are angry, we can make foolish decisions. Proverbs says anger can make us run around wild, having no self-control.

So, what are we supposed to do? None of us want to spend our lives angry, but it can feel impossible to overcome. God has made a way for us to escape the grip of anger.

Proverbs encourages us to ask God for patience and self-control. Without the protection of patience and self-control, we are like a city whose walls have been broken down by an invading army; our hearts are open for attack!

Back in the days of Solomon, if your city did not have thick, strong walls, you were an easy target for your enemies. The same is true of an unwise heart. If anger, rage, and hatred towards others are the enemy, then patience and self-control are the "walls of our city." If our walls are strong, we will enjoy peace even when frustrations come.

In the New Testament book of Romans, Paul writes that all of us were once enemies of God. We were the ones trying to tear down God's wall!

Why?

Our sin made us God's enemy. But God, in His patience, chose to love us. The Bible says that God sent Jesus to die for our sin, even though we had done nothing to deserve His love. Instead, Jesus died for us simply because God loves us. He chose to be patient with us. He put His anger at all our sin on His own Son instead of us.

When God did this, He destroyed the wall. Paul tells the Ephesians that because Jesus died for us, God has brought down the wall that separates us from Him. We are no longer enemies. We are His friends. Jesus's death was the punishment we deserved. Now we can be at peace with God.

We love because He first loved us. We can be patient and slow to anger because we have felt God's patience with us.

You deserve God's anger, but you get His love. Dwell on that. Let that truth shape us into people of wisdom.

FIGHTING

Most of us are familiar with the fruit of the Spirit: love, joy, peace, patience, kindness, goodness, faithfulness, gentleness, and self-control. We find the full list later in the Bible in Paul's letter to the Galatians.

Paul tells us that there is no law against any of these things. We can do them as much as we want and not get in trouble! But, Proverbs warns us that a life lived only for ourselves, and not others, will cause this fruit to be replaced with the rotten fruit of anger, argument, and fighting.

When we start to feel mad, it may not seem like a big deal at first. Solomon even says that someone who starts to argue is like a small crack in a large dam that holds back the waters of a river. The small leak will eventually become a large crack and the whole lake might surge through the dam! Likewise, anger and arguing leave lots of hurt in their paths!

We all know what the fruit of anger feels like, but what does its root look like? Proverbs tells us that arguing starts with foolishness.

Remember, the beginning of knowledge and wisdom is respect for the Lord. Respect for God causes us to treat others differently. We stop working just for ourselves and instead work for the good of others to build the kingdom of God. The opposite of this, of course, is foolishness. We lose all signs of the fruit of the Spirit when we become foolish.

Proverbs says it like this, "A person who isn't friendly looks out only for themselves. They are selfish and start fights. Foolish people are quick to argue."

So what do we do if we are in a fight? Proverbs gives a few solutions.

But know this: what you are about to read is not easy! It takes patience, kindness, and self-control, all fruits of the Spirit that come from God.

Proverbs tells us to stop "feeding the fire." If you keep adding wood to a fire, it will keep burning. Think of wood as insults or gossip. Words like these can be the fuel that keeps the fire of an argument going. So, learning to hold our tongues can calm a fight.

God also tells us to love our enemies. Proverbs says to give your enemy food if they are hungry and water if they grow thirsty. By doing this, you will do two things.

First, you may help the other person see how they are wrong, and lead them to apologize. It is hard to stay mad at someone who is loving you!

Second, your heart will probably soften as you serve. You may see how you were wrong, too!

All of this wisdom about bringing fights to an end reminds me of what God did for us.

God was angry. But not at us. He was angry at our sin. Now, God could have taken all His anger and kept "feeding the fire" by giving each person what their sin deserves - being separated from Him forever. But God didn't do that.

Instead of adding wood to the fire, He put His Son on a cross made of wood.

Jesus's cross ended the fight between God and us once and for all.

The Bible tells us over and over again that while we were enemies of God, Jesus died for us. We were spiritually hungry and thirsty. But instead of letting us suffer, He gave us food and drink.

Jesus is the bread of life. He is the living water.

This is the gospel - the good news! This is the way God shows us wisdom in action.

When we see what God did with His anger towards our sin, we can battle against our temptation to fight and instead love one another as God's children.

PRIDE

"You're a little too big for your britches."

I'm not sure where this old saying came from. And nobody calls pants "britches" anymore, right?! But it is a helpful picture.

Someone too big for their britches has suddenly swelled up to a size bigger than they used to be.

Pride does the same. When we grow proud, we think we are better than we really are. Pride makes us look down on others. We start to believe our smarts, skills, and stuff mean we are *really something else*!

The opposite of pride is humility. The Bible is full of opposites and things looking upside down. When we are proud and think we are high above people, Proverbs tells us we are actually on crumbling ground. But when we are humble and think of other people as better, we will be lifted up. Seems kind of backward, doesn't it?

Solomon says that a proud person is a fool who thinks everything is going great, but doesn't realize that they will be punished.

This is how the kingdom of God is so different from the world. Everything from school to sports will tell you to *be better*, *try harder*, and *do more*.

You should try hard. You should do your best. But, the kingdom of God says you do all of that to make your community and those around you better, not to puff yourself up!

Because God feels so strongly about the values of His kingdom, He says that He hates a proud heart and that those who have one will be punished.

That may seem a little harsh to our ears. I know I have often been known to have the "too big for my britches" disease! Is God going to punish me?

This is where Proverbs is such a great book. It points us to Jesus. If God only loves me when I become less prideful, then I am out of luck!

But if Jesus is the perfect wisdom of God, then He is the perfect picture of a pride-free life. After all, Jesus's life, from beginning to end, was humble.

He came into the world in a stinky stable. He was never rich. He never hung out with the cool kids, and He was not very well-liked by those in power. He was the opposite of proud!

You see, God's justice means our pride must be punished. But the good news of the gospel is that even though we're guilty, we are not the ones who receive the punishment. Jesus, the innocent one, does. Our pride is covered by His humble life.

When we grow in humility, we show others a picture of what Jesus is like. We become life-givers to those around us when we see, feel, and know that Jesus's humility saved us from death. Knowing that will help us make sure our britches always fit!

MARRIAGE

It might be hard to imagine, but one day if God wills it, you will be married. This may be weird to think about right now, and it might seem icky! Who would want to do that!? Live with a boy? Live with a girl? No thank you!

Marriage might also be a painful thought. Maybe your parents are not married anymore or were never married. That can be really hard.

Perhaps marriage is really challenging for your parents. Know that the Lord sees you and, in Jesus, has experienced all the pain of this world, including yours. He really knows how you feel!

Whatever the case may be, hide this knowledge deep in your heart for the right time!

First of all, what should you look for in a spouse? The Bible says the number one thing to find is someone who loves the Lord. You may find someone handsome, great to be around, or super funny, but Proverbs tells us that only goes so far. Solomon compares a beautiful woman who does not walk in wisdom to a gold ring in a pig's snout! The ring is gorgeous, but it is made ugly by what it's attached to. When it comes to picking a spouse, you can't compromise!

Spend lots of time getting to know the person you think God might call you to marry. Have fun with friends together. Talk about what's really important to you. The whole book of Proverbs could serve as a guide as you think about who you might marry. Are they growing in the ways the Bible celebrates or are they foolish? You might think about a few things in particular...

Solomon tells us that if you marry someone who loves to fight, they will be like rain dripping all day long. He even says that trying to stop a hot-tempered person is like trying to stop the wind! How impossible is that?!

A little arguing is good, and even healthy. But if someone likes to argue a lot, it will be miserable to live with them. Instead, look for someone whose words are "sweet like a honeycomb."

Instead of being a fighter, we should be quick to forgive. Solomon tells us that these kinds of people give life and love to those around them. The closer you live to someone, the more opportunities you have to love them. But the opposite is also true. You will have more chances to hurt one another, too. You want to be married to someone who treats you like God treats us: quick to forgive and slow to anger!

Be warned! The Bible says you need to love only one person the way you love your spouse. You are meant to care for them, be kind and generous to them, and remain loyal only to them.

But you may be tempted to treat more than one person like they are your spouse.

You might also convince yourself that it's okay. But loving anyone other than your spouse will harm you. Proverbs says that their words may seem smoother than oil and sweet like honey. But, in the end, this kind of relationship will leave a horrible taste in your mouth. This kind of empty love will be like a two-edged sword, destroying you to the core.

Keep far away from temptation like this. Do not even go near the door of their house or let their eyes capture you. Do not fool yourself into thinking you can "handle it." The Bible says this, "You can't shovel fire in your lap without burning your clothes!" You can't "play around" with evil. It will ruin you.

Instead, love your spouse and you will bring life to your family. Think of your spouse as a spring of water that is just for you and nobody else. If you treat your marriage in this way, you will be satisfied.

Now, why is marriage so important to God? The Bible says marriage reminds us of Jesus and the church. In fact, God calls the church "the bride of Christ."

Jesus loves His church, not because it is perfect, but because He chooses to. He loves the church so much that He died for her. He chose us to be His special people and is committed to us to the very end.

When we see marriages where both the husband and wife love one another with a committed and generous love, it reminds us of Jesus and how He loves the people of God. It models God's perfect and faithful love to the world.

So even if marriage seems icky now, hide these truths deep in your heart for your future self. If the Lord calls you to marriage one day, you'll need them!

PARENTS & KIDS

When God created Adam in the Garden, He said that man was not meant to live alone. God created Eve, and together Adam and Eve became the first parents. The rest of the Bible is full of stories about families and words of instruction for each member. Proverbs talks a lot to parents about the special role He designed for them.

But first, kids, Solomon also has some words for you. At the very beginning of the book of Proverbs we find this command: "Hear, my child, your father's instructions and don't forsake your mother's teachings."

The first thing you are supposed to do is simple - listen and obey.

While it sounds basic, listening to your mom and dad is a super important part of being wise. In fact, Proverbs says that if you stop listening to your parents, you've turned your back on wisdom and knowledge. You're headed in the completely wrong direction!

We all know that none of us obey our parents perfectly. Sometimes we will need to be corrected or disciplined. And believe it or not, that is a gift from God!

Your parents are obeying God and trying to help you in the way of wisdom. So Proverbs encourages us to not only put up with discipline, but to be thankful for it.

If we aren't able to have that attitude, we might be tempted to talk bad about or curse our parents. Solomon gives a strong warning that cursing your mom or dad will not end well for you. Destruction and ruin will come your way.

But in case you think the kids get the hardest message, Proverbs has a lot to say to parents too!

Solomon tells parents not to wait until you're older to start teaching you what is right and wrong. No, in fact, parents are supposed to start when you're a baby. Doing this will give you the greatest chance of having your best life.

But like we already said, we all are going to mess up. And parents sometimes have to discipline you. When done right, discipline doesn't make us scared of our parents or God. Instead, discipline helps us to know how to live with skill in a broken world.

Sometimes you might think your parents are just nagging you when they say, "You must clean your room! It is a royal mess!" Or, "You came home late from your friend's house; you must go to bed early tonight."

But what your parents or other adults, like teachers or pastors, are doing when they correct you is actually loving, even if it doesn't feel that way.

Proverbs tells us a person growing in wisdom gains more from a warning than a foolish person learns from being whipped 100 times. How is that possible?

A wise person sees the value in correction. They know they are not always right, and correction helps them grow into who God made them to be. So, instead of sticking our fingers in our ears when we are corrected, we need to give our full attention to those in authority.

Solomon says that when we do this, we start down the right path and grow in wisdom all the days of our lives.

Kids, you can encourage your parents! Tell them you want to grow in wisdom. Tell them you know that correction is a part of that. Work together and watch as you bloom!

Finally, parents can be a great blessing to a family. At the end of Proverbs, a mom is seen as someone who loves her family deeply. She speaks wisely, teaches faithfully, and watches over important family matters.

Her children adore her and call her "blessed." Her husband also praises her, saying, "Many women do excellent things. But you are better than all the others."

Fathers, too, bring joy to their families when they grow in wisdom and lead their children to honor the Lord. In the Bible, God says husbands are to be the life-giving leader of their families.

But you know that your parents are not perfect. They will make mistakes and need plenty of help from God. But God calls Himself our Father. Your parents love you, but it's not enough. Every one of us longs for a parent to love us perfectly.

Our parents offer a dim reflection of God's love and all of us, on our best and worst days, can rest in His perfect, fatherly love.

FRIENDS

There's a magnet on our refrigerator that reads, "Friends are the family you choose." Isn't that true? You can't control who your parents are or how many brothers and sisters you have. But, you do get a lot of say over who becomes a friend.

Proverbs says we become like the people we spend time with. If our friends have a terrible temper, we will probably grow a short fuse as well. If our friends are self-controlled, we will likely learn to think carefully about what we say and do.

When you have a big decision, who do you talk to? The older you get, the more you'll likely talk to your friends about important things. If your friends are faithful to God and loyal to you, they can be a great source of wisdom.

But the opposite is also true. Proverbs says if your friends do not walk with God and do not have your best interests in mind, they can cause pain in your life that feels like a broken tooth. Yikes! That hurts just thinking about it!

Proverbs tells us that wise friends will hurt us too, but it's a good type of hurt! When you ask a faithful friend for advice, what they say may be painful first. It may not be what you want to hear, and they may even have to correct you or point out sin. But your friend cares about you. They want you to become more like Jesus in every way.

That is real love!

However, when you ask an unwise friend for advice, it can go very differently. They will tell you what you want to hear. They may even kiss up to you. In fact, Proverbs says that very thing.

Solomon says that the words of the foolish may feel more like kisses. But they are not looking out for you. They just want you to like them.

But a wise friend cares about making your life better. Just like perfume makes a room smell better, they refresh you through and through. They add a sweet presence to your life.

The sweet perfume of friendship gives us a hint that Jesus is near. In fact, Jesus told His disciples that He called them friends!

Proverbs whispers to us about Jesus's friendship when Solomon says things like, "there is a friend who sticks closer than a brother," and, "a friend loves at all times and is there for you when trouble comes."

Jesus does what no other friend would do. John tells us later in the Bible that the greatest love is when you are willing to lay down your life for a friend. Jesus willingly did this for you! His love for us can shape our hearts and lives so that we are the best friends anyone could ever ask for.

God gives us the gift of friendship to grow our wisdom, help us enjoy life, and to show us more and more of His friendship to us in Jesus.

GRIEF & DEATH

Life does not always bring us joy and smiles. Sometimes it is filled with sorrow and sadness. We feel down when friends move to a new town. When someone in our family gets sick, it can make us downright gloomy. You may have even had a pet die. Those days are always sad!

Life is hard. But the Bible says there is joy to be had even in sadness. In fact, God can use difficult circumstances for our good. How so?

God wants to give us good gifts here on earth. He wants us to experience the beauty this world has to offer. But He also wants our hearts to look forward to the best gifts found in heaven.

Proverbs tells us that our hearts long for a love that will never end. That longing makes sickness, loss, grief, and death even sadder. But our losses here on earth make heaven all the more glorious!

Imagine experiencing painless, sorrowless happiness that never ends and sharing it with the One who made you!

But until then, we trust the Lord. He sent His own Son to earth to know our sorrows and feel our pain. God may not give us answers for why cancer and skinned knees happen, but He knows what those things feel like. He understands our pain, and that makes him the best comforter.

Suffering and sadness are things we all experience. The Bible helps us know how to love our friends who are suffering. Proverbs reminds us that we can be helpful just by listening to those who are sad.

Solomon explains that each heart knows its own sadness. We cannot pretend to understand all that someone is going through when they have a death in their family or are really sick. But we can listen to their pain. We can sit with them and let them know that they are not alone.

Sometimes we may want to rush a friend right past their grief. We might tell them to stop crying or just think of something happy. We may think we're helping, but that can just make it worse. Proverbs reminds us that you can sing happy songs to a heavy and troubled heart, but that is really insensitive. It causes more pain in the end.

Telling your friend that everything is ok when it's not can be like taking their coat away on a cold day. It's just plain wrong. You aren't offering comfort at all!

Instead, we can simply sit with our friends in their pain. Paul tells us in the book of Romans to rejoice with those who are joyful and to be sad with those who are sad. Likewise, Proverbs says it is ok to be sad and to be a friend to someone grieving a loss.

Change can bring loss too. As we grow older, a lot of things start to change. One day, many, many years from now, your body won't be so young anymore. It's hard to imagine, I know! But, when you are older, you'll want to remember this.

One day in the future, you won't be able to run as fast, and you may even start to forget more things than you remember! Even still, growing old is not something to fight against; rather, it is to be celebrated. Our world may say that growing old is bad, but the Bible says it has a lot of value.

Proverbs says it like this, "Gray hair is a glorious crown and brings honor to old men."

When you are young, you might be proud of your strength. As you grow older, your muscles will shrink, but you'll grow stronger in something more important - wisdom.

And then one day, what happens to all people will happen to you. Death may come when you are old and frail. It may also come sooner. But even though death is sad, it is nothing to fear. Instead, Proverbs tells us we can find safety in God even as we die.

When we die, we lose everything we have here on earth. But we gain everything our hearts always longed for in heaven - a love that will never end.

And the good news is that the thing we can never lose, God's love, we can have now. We can know we are safe forever by trusting that Jesus lost everything when He died on the cross so He could gain us forever. He defeated death, and we can trust that we can and will live forever with Him.

JUSTICE

When God calls us to be His children, we are welcomed into a beautiful community. Instead of only looking out for our own wants and needs, we also think about what's best for others.

Proverbs tells us that all people have one thing in common. All of us were made in God's image. That means that everyone, everywhere is worthy of what the Bible calls *justice*.

What is justice? It's a word we don't often use. But we know it when we see it - and when we don't. Justice, or acting justly, means treating others fairly. It means following the rules in a way that brings about peace for all people, not just a chosen few.

Justice reminds us that everyone is valuable to God. Justice requires that those who do wrong be held responsible. God's justice demands that our sins be punished. But in His mercy, God sent Jesus to die in our place and take the punishment we deserve.

You and I do not get the penalty our sin deserves. What amazingly good news! When we grow in the wisdom of justice, we see God's love for us and the world more clearly.

The Bible tells us that everyone is worthy of dignity and respect. So, when people are unjustly mistreated, it should break our hearts because it's against God's plan for how the world is supposed to work.

God's plan is far more beautiful! When Jesus returns and the world is made perfect again, it will be so peaceful that lions and lambs become friends instead of enemies. In God's kingdom, people lay down their weapons and seek understanding instead of war.

How can you be a person who works to bring justice to the world? Proverbs gives us lots of ideas!

At any age, you can speak up for those who have a harder time speaking up for themselves. Sometimes our world tends to forget about the poor and powerless. But the Bible says that is not right. Instead, we should have eyes to see those who are poor and oppressed and move towards them in love.

This sounds a lot like what God does for us! He turned towards us in love when He could have forgotten us.

How could you be the hands and feet of God in this way? Perhaps your family could write a note of encouragement to someone who needs it. Maybe you could help everyone follow the rules during a game or make sure toys are shared evenly with friends.

Proverbs also talks a lot about rulers. Today we might think of rulers as leaders like presidents, queens, and prime ministers. But a leader is anyone who has been put in charge of a group of people. That includes school principles, pastors, and coaches, too.

We should pray for our leaders and encourage them. The job of a leader is very challenging! We can pray that they lead in ways that are fair and loving to all people. We can pray they act justly and live rightly.

If God causes our leaders to gain wisdom, they can bless many people! For instance, Solomon writes that when leaders speak the right words at the right time, it can be like golden apples in silver jewelry - stunningly beautiful and valuable!

Finally, Proverbs teaches us that being people of justice means doing what is right, even when those around us do not. Solomon writes, "Whoever says to the wicked, 'You are right,' is like a muddied spring or a polluted fountain."

Agreeing with people who break God's law might help you fit in for a moment, but it will make a mess of your life and confuse your understanding of truth.

As God's image-bearers, we should feel angry and sad when we see evil in the world. God does not like what the wicked do, and we should not either. When we see evil, we should do what we can to stop it. We should act justly.

Why do we do all of this? Doing the right thing, stopping evil, and speaking up for others is not easy. Plus, it doesn't always turn out the way we want!

God knows this. And it won't always be this way.

One day, evil will finally meet its end.

In the New Testament book of Revelation, John tells us that all wars, diseases, and evil will be destroyed when Jesus returns. But, all of those who follow Jesus will see Him on His throne as the perfect leader and judge.

God will destroy everything wicked and protect His children.

When that day comes, there will be no need to fight for justice. Everything will be the way it's supposed to be, and people from every walk of life will gather around the throne of God, praising Him forever.

Today, as we work alongside God to create justice, we give ourselves and others a sneak preview of what heaven will be like: full of the true wisdom of God, in Jesus.

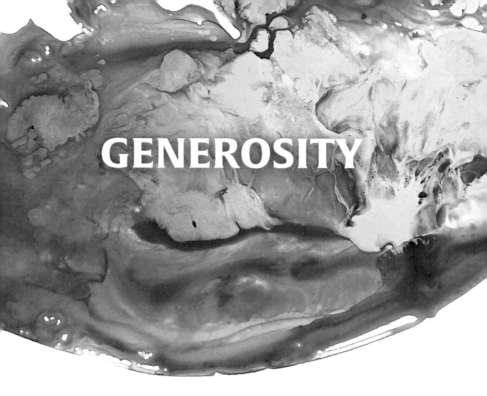

GENEROSITY

God made all things. That one truth is like a piece of thread you can pull all the way through the fabric of the Bible. That one truth changes everything.

Famously, Psalm 24 says, "The earth belongs to God and everything it contains." God made it all. God owns it all. And then, He trusts people like us to care for all He created. Why does God do that?

You see, another thread that weaves through the Scriptures is that you and I have been adopted as sons and daughters of God. We have been brought into God's family!

Jesus talks a lot about this new family. He says that God is the best father. He knows how to give the best gifts to His children!

And because God made it all and owns it all, when He gives to His children, He does so generously! God gives us everything we need and sometimes even more.

Now, get this. God doesn't sit around waiting for us to do good things or pray big prayers before He provides for us. Sometimes God gives us more when we already have plenty.

Proverbs tells us that a part of learning to be wise is knowing what to do when God gives us more than we need. Whether it is money, space, time, food, or love, how we treat our *extra* is extra important!

When we give away what God has given us, we show people more of God and grow in generosity. In fact, when we are generous, we live the way we were made to, reflecting God's image to the world!

To become generous people, the Bible says we need to build new habits and ways of living. As funny as it may sound, that reminds me of my childhood guinea pig.

I named her Queen (after the band...ask your parents). The first few weeks after we brought Queen home from the pet store, she had an uncontrollable appetite. She grew, and grew, and grew; perhaps much more quickly and rounder than the average guinea pig!

One day, all of that changed. I went out on the porch to feed Queen and was in for quite the surprise.

There was not just one guinea pig anymore! Overnight, Queen gave birth to two baby boys! She had been pregnant the whole time!

After Queen weaned the boys off mama's milk, we noticed a change in her. She no longer ate every piece of food in her bowl. Instead, she saved some for her children.

This story of Queen reminds me of what the Bible values. We look out for the needs of others just as we would look out for our own needs. Queen now had children, and she was constantly thinking about them and what she could do to help them grow. Life wasn't all about her anymore!

God celebrates generosity whenever He sees it. Throughout the Old Testament, farmers were told to leave the edges of their fields unharvested. This allowed the poor to gather food. Solomon noticed the wisdom in this by saying that people who are kind to those in need honor the Lord.

In contrast to the Old Testament farmers, Proverbs tells us that foolish people eat up everything they have. People growing in wisdom, however, do not "live to the edges of their fields." We shouldn't take and use all we have just for ourselves.

Today this might mean that we don't spend all of our time doing only what we want to do. Instead, we set aside time to serve others. When we plan to be generous, we will look for opportunities to bless God's people.

But what if we give away too much? Can you be too generous?

Wisdom tells us to provide for our family first and not take away what they need for life. But generosity often surprises us by not leaving us with less, but by blessing us with more. When we are generous with what we have, it is like we are agreeing with God by saying with our heart and hands, "I know that God will provide what I need."

How will God lead you to be generous? Perhaps it starts by looking at what He has given you each day. It could be energy or time. Maybe it's extra food in your lunch box or knowledge of something difficult in school.

Thank God for these good gifts! He is the maker of time, the provider of food, and the one who gave you understanding. Without Him, you would not have all that you have.

Then, ask God to help you know how to use your *extra*. Maybe one of your teachers needs help carrying something. Perhaps your friend forgot his lunch, and you can share yours. Or you see someone struggling at school and can offer some encouraging help.

Get your family in on the fun too! Invite new friends over for dinner or save up money together to support a cause near to your heart.

And then, smile! God is working through you! If you build a habit of generosity when you are young, you will leave a trail of joy behind you all the days of your life.

We should ask ourselves, what motivates our generosity? Am I just trying to be good, or am I responding to God's generosity to me?

Remember, the whole book of Proverbs points to Jesus. God saw our need. But we didn't just forget our lunch. No, we were dead in our sins!

Because of our sin, we were separated from God. We needed a rescuer! Instead of giving us what we deserve, God gave His own Son to die in our place. Jesus gave His life so we could receive eternal life with Him.

We can never outgive God. But, we can show the world more of His generosity when we freely give what He has given to us. We love because God first loved us. We are generous because God gave us the greatest gift the world has ever known.

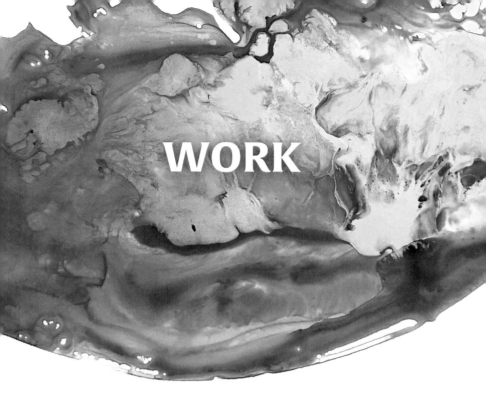

WORK

If you ask me, Adam and Eve had a great life in the Garden of Eden. Picture it with me.

God made the whole world out of nothing. All the streams, meadows, horses, mountains, and everything in between. Everything was perfect!

Then, God asked Adam and Eve to take care of His creation. In a sense, He gave them a job and made them His first workers.

"Name the animals. Grow the plants. Love my world!"

What a fantastic life!

Work. It's a part of creation. God is a worker. Adam and Eve were called to be workers, too. Work was made to be delightful and soul-satisfying.

But (and that's a really big BUT), Satan came and messed up everything! When Adam and Eve disobeyed and ate of the tree in the garden, everything instantly changed about their work. The crops grew thorns; they began to sweat when they harvested the fields, and work, as they knew it, changed forever.

Speaking of thorns, Proverbs says the way of those who don't want to work is blocked with thorns. Sounds a lot like what happened in the garden, right?

Now, work is not just what our parents do when they go to their offices. Everyone works. Babies work to learn how to crawl. You probably work at school, in your friendships, at your church, or on your basketball team. Wherever you go, whatever you do, you are making something of God's world, and you are - you guessed it - working! But work, as you know, isn't always fun and easy.

I remember a time in school when I was not doing well in my math class. My teacher looked at me and said, "Chris, I know you're smart. But you are lazy!"

She was right. One way sin changes our work is that we can grow lazy. Proverbs tells us that when we feel this way, we should look down. Not at the leaves or pine needles, but at something much, much smaller.

The ants.

Ants have no commander, leader, or ruler, but they work hard building their homes and gathering food. Sure, they may take a little rest here and there, but an ant is always busy being the best ant it can be!

The Bible says we can learn a lot from ants. God made you to work hard as you bring life to the places you visit and the people you see. He wants you to work alongside others doing your unique part. He doesn't want you to try to do everything yourself or carry a big burden. But He does want you to be diligent and do everything for His glory.

However you're gifted to work, know this: God made you in His image! That means you are a reflection of God everywhere you go as you carry out the unique work He gives you.

One day, you will be big and grown-up. Then, you may have a career that pays money. This work is not more important than other types of work people do, like taking care of babies or mowing the grass. God values all work.

But, if you have this type of work, you'll want to make sure you take good care of the money God provides for you. Money, after all, does not last forever. So, save some of it for times when you might not be able to work or for when you are ready to retire. Planning for the future shows wisdom in our work!

Make sure that when you have a job one day, whether it is on a construction site or in a hospital, that you do it well. As Christians, we do not merely work for man, but for God. We work hard to honor our bosses and co-workers and provide for our families.

Always remember this: whoever you are, wherever you go, God has work for you to do. It is wise to find the work God has gifted you to do and then go for it with all your heart, soul, mind, and strength!

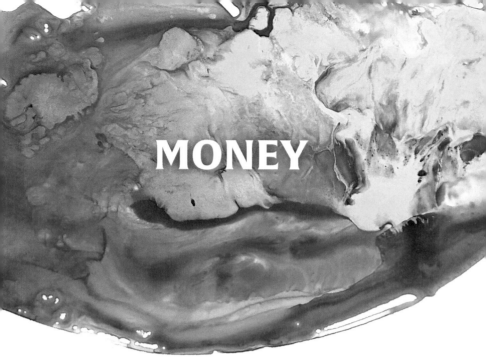

MONEY

Is money a tool or a treasure? What's the difference?

A tool is something that helps us get what we need. Keys open doors. Saws cut wood. Hammers drive nails. Cars move people. Cups hold water.

Treasures are something quite different. They can be precious to one person but mean nearly nothing to someone else.

Photos of my children are treasures to me. If a fire erupted in our house, they would be some of the first things I'd save. But I doubt that pictures of my children would mean much to you. In fact, you might think it quite silly to watch me run into a burning house just to save a few pieces of paper!

Treasures are like that, though. Their importance is not wrapped around our brains, but instead take hold of our hearts. This is why money gets dangerous.

The writer of Proverbs asks God to make him neither poor nor rich, but only to give him the bread he needs for the day. Why? The writer knows if he has too much bread, he might think he doesn't need God. But he also knows that if there's too little bread, he might steal from others and dishonor God's name.

This is why money is a great tool, but a horrible treasure. If you want it too much, it may take over your heart and become like a god to you. And money, as it turns out, is a horrible god to worship.

Solomon explains that riches are here one day and gone the next. He paints the picture of riches growing wings and flying away like an eagle.

Instead of wanting riches, Solomon says, you should want a good name. It is better to be highly respected in your family and amongst your friends. In fact, Proverbs says that to be respected is better than having silver or gold!

How do we gain this respect when it comes to money? First, we take care of the people around us. Don't take advantage of the poor just so you can make more money. The Bible says it is better to be poor and live without blame than to follow a crooked path to get rich.

Second, you should desire to gain wisdom more than riches. We honor the Lord with all our heart, mind, soul, and strength. Then, if riches come, we use wisdom before the Lord to care for our families and bless one another.

A rich person may think they are wise because they have money. But a poor person who has gained understanding knows that those who gathered wealth without honoring the Lord are foolish and empty.

Just so you don't think all this talk of *treasure* is something I made up, the Bible actually uses this same word. In the Gospel of Matthew, Jesus tells His disciples not to store up treasure on earth because moths and rust can destroy it.

Just a few lines later, Jesus says something similar, but also stronger, "You cannot serve two masters. Either God or money can be your master, but you cannot have it both ways. One of them has to win."

This is why money is tricky. It's a tool we all need. Yet it also has superpowers that can fool you into thinking it's a treasure. We might start to think money can meet needs that only God can.

But God is kind enough to show us a better way. In the New Testament book of Galatians, Paul says that we have been called children of God. In Biblical times, being a child meant that all your father owned would one day become yours.

Paul goes on to say that because we are called children of God, we no longer have to answer to other masters. Instead, we can call God our master and our Father and know that everything He has is ours. Money does not need to be our master.

We can trust that God will care for us. We have no need to worry about what we'll wear, what we'll eat, or if we'll have enough money. God gives the birds food and clothes the flowers. But birds and flowers are not God's children. We are!

He chose to call Himself our loving Father. He knows our needs and takes care of us. God made us His treasure so that He would become our treasure as well.

PLANS

Picture in your mind a beautiful day. The sun is out, the birds are chirping, and there isn't a cloud in sight. What do you want to do?

Perhaps you'd like to go to the park, run around, ride down the slides over and over, and then top it all off with a delicious popsicle. What a fantastic day that would be! You ready to get in the car? Let's go!

But, as soon as you finish putting on your shoes, you hear it...thunder. Then the pitter-patter of rain.

Just a few moments ago, it looked like the perfect day. And now? Well, plans changed.

Life rarely goes how we planned it. Even today, as I am writing this, I was supposed to meet a friend for lunch. They just called to cancel. What will I do for lunch? My tummy is already grumbling!

Proverbs tells us that it's actually a good thing to have plans. But, the key to wise planning is to make sure we hold those plans with a loose grip and allow God to lead. That, however, is much easier said than done!

But wisdom tells us to believe that God really does have everything under control and that He is not surprised by the things that surprise us.

The book of Proverbs says that nothing can get in the way of God's plan. That means we can make plans all we want, but God can make things happen like rain and canceled lunches that totally change what we had in mind.

God doesn't do that because He is mean and wants to take all the fun away. In fact, He directs our plans for our good and His glory.

Solomon writes that nobody can understand their own ways because it is the Lord who directs our steps. On this side of heaven, we may never know why rain suddenly falls on a perfect day. But God has a reason, and we can trust Him.

So what do we do? The Bible tells us that, most of the time, the plans of people who work hard succeed. Of course, we know that you can work really hard and still fall flat on your face!

The Bible also says that not planning can keep you from success. But, again, there are plenty of people who didn't start with a good plan but God chose to bless them anyway!

So which is it? Do we make plans for our lives? What do we want to be when we grow up? Where do we want to live? What sport should we play this season?

Proverbs tells us to make plans *and* still let the Lord lead. We shouldn't become so set in our plans that we lose heart when God has something different in mind. We also shouldn't be lazy, not plan, and have nothing to do.

Think of it this way. Solomon says a wise person has a heart like a stream of water. You can change the flow of a stream with a pile of rocks or a log just as rain can change your plans. But the water, and we, will keep on going.

What should we do when God changes our plans? Let's go back to our perfect park day. Of course, we would be upset. After all, it was going to be such a great day! But, as we watch the rain fall, we can trust that God's plan is best. Then we can think of something new to do and thank God that He has everything under control.

After all, weird plans are the story of the Bible. If we were to have written the Bible's story, we would have never planned for a helpless baby to save the world. I sincerely doubt we would have made Jesus come from a poor family and have stinky fishermen as best friends!

But God's unusual plan was way better than anything we could have come up with on our own. If we can trust God with His plan to save the whole world, then we can certainly trust him with what he has for our lives!

ONE LAST WORD

This has been fun! The book of Proverbs is full God's wonderful wisdom, and I hope you have been encouraged.

If you have trusted Jesus, you have the Holy Spirit living inside you. So, if you have seen hints of wisdom in your life already, I'm not surprised. God is at work!

Perhaps you have also been challenged. None of us have mastered wisdom. We all need to continue growing in our love for God and others throughout our lives. I hope God has shown you some areas where you'd like to ask the Lord to help you grow.

Most of all, I hope you've seen Jesus. He is on every page of your Bible. As Sally Lloyd-Jones writes in the *Jesus Storybook Bible,* "Every story whispers His name." I hope you see that Proverbs is just as much about Jesus as any book in the Bible.

Towards the end of Proverbs, Solomon says, "Some people are pure in their own eyes. But they are still covered in all their filth and sin."

Do you think of yourself as being a good person? You might be kind and generous, but the Bible tells us that God won't love us if we are just *good*. We have to be *perfect*.

The only person God sees as perfect is Jesus.

But, if you make Jesus the Lord of your life by confessing your sin and asking for His forgiveness, God looks at you like he looks at Jesus...*perfect*.

The true wisdom of God is Jesus. And the only way to eternal life is to tell God about your sins and receive His forgiveness.

When we trade the *good* life for His *perfect* life, you will see that Jesus is better than gold!

SCRIPTURE INDEX

Below are places you can go in your Bible to learn more about wisdom! All of these passages were woven into *Better Than Gold*.

WISDOM & FOOLISHNESS
Proverbs 1:1-9; 2:1-15; 27:22

TWO PATHS
Proverbs 4:14-19

TWO MEALS
Proverbs 1:20-33; 8:1-9:18

HONOR THE LORD
Proverbs 8:13; 14:26-27; 15:3; 15:16; 15:33; 19:23, 28:14, 29:25

KNOWLEDGE

Proverbs 15:4; 15:21; 16:20; 16:22; 17:27; 23:12

CREATION

Proverbs 8:22-31

WORDS

Proverbs 4:24; 6:17; 8:8; 8:13; 10:11; 10:19; 10:21; 10:30-31; 11:9; 11:13; 12:13-14; 12:18-19; 12:22; 13:2-3; 14:4; 15:1-4; 15:14; 15:26; 15:28; 16:21; 16:23-24; 18:4; 18:8; 18:21; 20:15; 21:23; 25:15; 26:24-26; 26:28; 29:20

HONESTY

Proverbs 6:16-20; 10:9 11:3; 12:22; 16:13; 16:17; 16:28; 19:5; 19:9; 19:28; 20:10; 20:17; 21:29; 22:29; 23:10-11; 24:26

ANGER

Proverbs 14:17; 14:29; 14:30; 15:13; 15:15; 15:18; 16:32; 25:28; 27:3-4; 27:19; 29:11

FIGHTING

Proverbs 15:18; 16:32; 17:14; 17:19; 18:1; 18:6; 18:18; 20:2-3; 20:22; 22:10; 24:28-29; 25:21-22; 26:17; 26:20-21; 29:8; 29:22

PRIDE

Proverbs 14:6; 15:12; 15:25; 16:5; 16:18; 18:12-13; 21:24; 22:4; 29:23; 30:32

MARRIAGE

Proverbs 2:16-19; 5:3-23; 6:23; 7:4; 11:22; 12:4; 14:1; 15:1; 15:6; 17:1; 18:22; 19:13-14; 21:9; 21:19; 22:1; 22:14; 23:27; 25:24; 27:15-17

PARENTS & KIDS
Proverbs 6:20; 13:24; 14:26; 15:5; 15:20; 17:6; 17:10; 17:21; 19:13; 19:18; 19:20; 19:26-27; 20:7; 22:6; 22:15; 23:13-14; 23:22-25; 29:15; 29:17; 31:26-31

FRIENDS
Proverbs 14:7; 15:22; 17:9; 17:17; 18:19; 18:24; 22:24-25; 23:19-21; 25:19; 27:6; 27:9-10; 27:17

GRIEF & DEATH
Proverbs 14:10; 14:13; 14:32; 16:31; 20:29; 25:20

JUSTICE
Proverbs 11:26; 21:15; 22:22-23; 24:24-25; 25:11-12; 28:16; 29:13; 31:8-9

GENEROSITY
Proverbs 11:24; 14:21; 14:31; 19:17; 21:19-20; 28:27

WORK
Proverbs 6:6-11; 10:4-5; 12:11; : 12:14; 13:11; 14:23; 15:19; 18:9; 19:15; 19:24; 20:4; 21:6; 22:13; 24:27; 26:13-16; 27:23-27; 28:19; 30:25-26

MONEY
Proverbs 1:19; 11:25-26; 13:22; 14:20; 14:24; 22:1; 22:9; 22:16; 23:4-5; 27:23-24; 28:6; 28:8; 28:11; 28:27; 30:8

PLANS
Proverbs 16:1-4; 16:9; 19:21; 20:24; 21:1; 21:5; 21:30-31